GREAT OUTDOORS
SPORTS ZONE

WATERFOWL
HUNTING DUCK, GOOSE, AND MORE
Tom Carpenter

Lerner Publications Company • Minneapolis

Lerner Publications Company

A division of Lerner Publishing Group, Inc.

241 First Avenue North

Minneapolis, MN 55401 U.S.A.

Website address: www.lernerbooks.com

Content Consultant: James G. Dickson, PhD, wildlife biologist, researcher, author, professor, and hunter

Library of Congress Cataloging-in-Publication Data

Carpenter, Tom, 1962–

    Waterfowl hunting : duck, goose, and more / by Tom Carpenter.

       p. cm. — (Great outdoors sports zone)

    Includes index.

    ISBN 978–1–4677–0221–8 (lib. bdg. : alk. paper)

    1. Waterfowl shooting—Juvenile literature. I. Title.

  SK331.C366 2013

  799.2'44—dc23   2012002263

Manufactured in the United States of America
1—CG—7/15/12

The images in this book are used with the permission of: Backgrounds: © ElementalImaging/iStockphoto; © Andrew Howe/iStockphoto; © Patrimonio Designs Limited/Shutterstock Images; © Suzi Nelson/Shutterstock Images, p. 5; © Ted Thai/Time Life Pictures/Getty Images, p. 6; © Library of Congress, pp. 7 (LC-USZ62-46999), 8 (LC-DIG-pga-01748), 9 (LC-USZC2-6216); © Erwin and Peggy Bauer/USFWS, pp. 10–11; © Chelsi Hornbaker/USFWS, p. 11; © Donna Dewhurst/USFWS, pp. 12, 27 (top); © Lauren Victoria Burke/AP Images, p. 13; © Jon Larson/iStockphoto, p. 14; © Red Line Editorial, pp. 15, 23 (top), 29; © Eric Von Seggern/Shutterstock Images, p. 16; © Nigel Dowsett/Shutterstock Images, p. 17 (top); © Richard Semik/Shutterstock Images, p. 17 (bottom); © Dan Bannister/Shutterstock Images, p. 18 (top); © Risteski Goce/Shutterstock Images, p. 18 (bottom); © Ryan Howe/iStockphoto, p. 19; © Mike Hemming/USFWS, p. 20; © Jens Stolt/Shutterstock Images, p. 21; © Andy Gehrig/iStockphoto, p. 22; © Daniel Alvarez/Shutterstock Images, p. 23 (bottom); © Jens Stolt/Shutterstock Images, p. 24; © USFWS, pp. 25, 26 (bottom); © Melinda Fawver/Shutterstock Images, p. 26 (top); © FloridaStock/Shutterstock Images, p. 26 (middle); © Lee Karney/USFWS, p. 27 (top middle); © Miao Liao/Shutterstock Images, p. 27 (bottom middle); © Vishnevskiy Vasily/Shutterstock Images, p. 27 (bottom); © a9photo/Shutterstock Images, p. 28. Front cover: © David Wei/Alamy.

Main body text set in Avenir LT Std 65 Medium 11/17.
Typeface provided by Adobe Systems.

TABLE OF CONTENTS

WHY HUNT WATERFOWL?

CHAPTER ONE

Combining bird hunting and water can be lots of fun! Waterfowl are birds, such as ducks or geese, that live in or near water. These birds live in wetlands and other wet areas with shallow water. Rivers, creeks, ponds, and lakes also attract waterfowl. Ducks and geese are sometimes hunted on land, where they stop to feed in fields.

These wild birds might seem easy to find. You have probably seen them by the side of the road or even in your backyard. But hunting ducks and geese takes hard work and skill. First of all, this type of game hunting means getting out of bed early. Hunters wait in hiding spots called blinds. When the sky gets light enough to shoot by, it is almost time to hunt!

Hunting geese and ducks is a great way to get outdoors and spend time with an older friend or family member. Most hunters don't measure hunting success by the number of ducks or geese they've killed. True success is getting out in the marsh and enjoying the hunt.

Waterfowl hunting is an exciting way to get out in nature.

CHAPTER TWO

HISTORY OF WATERFOWL HUNTING

Humans have been hunting and eating North American waterfowl for as long as they have lived on the continent. Native Americans depended on these birds to feed their families. These early hunters shot ducks and geese with bows and arrows.

Native Americans used decoys (fake ducks) in their hunting. In 1924, 2,000-year-old duck decoys made of wetland plants were found in Nevada.

Native Americans used canoes to get closer to the waterfowl they were hunting.

Native Americans also used traps and nets. They built traps from sticks they tied together. Ducks could swim into these traps but couldn't get out. Hunters sometimes would sneak up on ducks and throw a net over them. They used boats or canoes made from wood or from woven wetland plants to get closer to waterfowl.

In the 1800s, settlers hunted for sport as well as for food and resources.

Europeans Arrive

When European settlers started to arrive in North America in the 1500s, the numbers of waterfowl seemed endless. Settlers hunted ducks and geese every month of the year. Later, hunters discovered that markets in cities would buy ducks and geese. As a result, market hunting was born.

Market Hunting

Market hunting was a business, not a sport. A market hunter wanted to bag (shoot and collect) as many birds as possible. Harvested ducks were put on ice and brought to markets in the city where people bought the meat and feathers.

Over time, market hunting hurt waterfowl populations. As settlers spread across North America, cities and farm fields spread. These settled places took over waterfowl habitats. With so much of their habitats destroyed and so many shot for market, these bird populations were in danger. Something had to be done.

These duck hunters in 1899 may have sold their ducks to markets in the city.

CHAPTER THREE

PROTECTING DUCKS AND GEESE

In modern times, waterfowl populations are stronger than they used to be. Each U.S. state has fish and game agencies. These agencies manage and protect waterfowl and other wildlife. Many conservation organizations also work to protect these birds. Conservation is the smart use of natural resources.

Hunting Seasons

The U.S. Fish and Wildlife Service sets certain hunting season rules. Each state's fish and game agency then sets hunting seasons and bag limits based on the national hunting rules.

Duck populations are no longer in danger because regulations keep hunters from overhunting.

Scientists and conservationists band waterfowl, such as this Canada goose, to track their populations.

Managing waterfowl is different for each state because ducks and geese migrate (move around). In the summer, the birds may fly to cooler places. In the winter, they may fly to areas with warmer weather.

The rules vary, but most states allow a 60-day duck season each fall and winter and a 107-day goose season. Some states split the season to take advantage of different duck and goose migrations. A state might have an early season for teal ducks, which migrate early; a regular season for all ducks; and a late season for northern mallards, which migrate last.

Some states have bag limits on how many females a hunter can take from a certain kinds of ducks. Hunters must learn to tell male and female ducks apart.

Bag Limits

A bag limit is how many ducks or geese a hunter can shoot in a single day. Bag limits protect species (kinds) of ducks from overhunting. For example, you might be able to bag six ducks per day but only one canvasback, and two scaup. Read your state's hunting rules closely and obey them!

Duck Stamps

Adults who hunt ducks are required to buy a U.S. Migratory Bird Hunting and Conservation Stamp (usually known as a duck stamp). This stamp acts as a hunting license. Most stamp money goes directly to buying and improving waterfowl habitats throughout the country. Most states also have their own duck stamp. These stamps raise millions of dollars each year. The stamps help the states manage other kinds of wetland wildlife too, not just ducks and geese.

WATERFOWL CONSERVATION

What can you do to help ducks and geese?

- Buy a duck stamp even if you don't have to.

- Join a conservation organization such as Ducks Unlimited (DU) or Delta Waterfowl.

- Obey the laws set up to protect waterfowl populations.

- Focus on trying for drakes (male birds) when you hunt. Save the hens (female birds) for raising young birds.

Conservation organizations are important to waterfowl's future. Ducks Unlimited (DU) and Delta Waterfowl are two well-known organizations that support waterfowl hunting. They work to protect waterfowl and their habitats. Many of these organizations' members are hunters. These members donate their time and money to wildlife habitat projects that benefit waterfowl.

MIGRATORY BIRD HUNTING AND CONSERVATION STAMP

$15

Void after June 30, 2006

Hooded Merganser

U.S. DEPARTMENT OF THE INTERIOR

A duck stamp can't be used for postage. But it does act as your hunting license.

CHAPTER FOUR

BE A SAFE HUNTER

Any kind of hunting is a big responsibility. You must look out for your own safety and the safety of other people, hunting dogs, and property. Firearms safety is especially important. You must buy a hunting license. Learn the boundaries of the land where you are hunting. You need to follow all hunting rules and regulations. You also must make sure that you are hunting in a way that is humane, or fair and considerate to the animal.

It is your job to learn how to hunt safely before going out in the field.

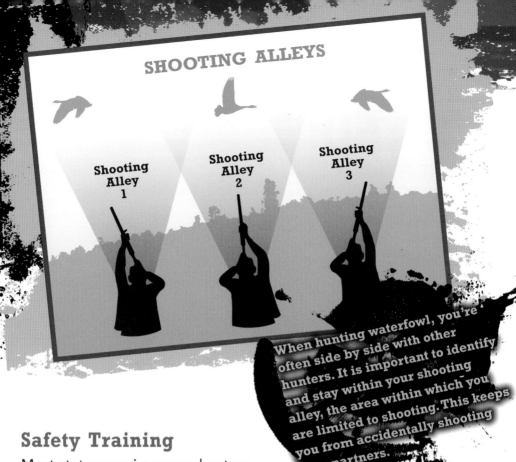

SHOOTING ALLEYS

Shooting
Alley
1

Shooting
Alley
2

Shooting
Alley
3

When hunting waterfowl, you're often side by side with other hunters. It is important to identify and stay within your shooting alley, the area within which you are limited to shooting. This keeps you from accidentally shooting your partners.

Safety Training

Most states require young hunters to take a firearms or a hunting safety course. Not only is this the law, but it is also a smart idea. In a safety course, you will learn the techniques for hunting safely so that you don't shoot or injure yourself or a fellow hunter.

FIREARMS SAFETY

Here is the basic formula for gun safety. Remember these letters: TAB-K.

- **T**reat every firearm as if it were loaded.
- **A**lways point the muzzle (tip of the gun) in a safe direction.
- **B**e sure of your target and what lies beyond it.
- **K**eep on the safety (a device that prevents accidental firing), and keep your finger off the trigger until you are

Where to Hunt

All state game agencies list public hunting lands on their websites. If you're not sure the land is public, don't hunt there.

Successful waterfowl hunting often happens on private land, such as farmland. As a hunter, you are responsible for getting permission to hunt on private land. Be courteous when you ask to hunt. Show the landowner you are a responsible hunter. And thank the landowner after your hunt. That way the spot could be yours to use in the future too!

Hunting Regulations

When hunting, you need to follow all regulations. With waterfowl hunting, these rules change each year. Not knowing a law is not an excuse to break it! You can get regulations booklets at sporting goods stores, state offices, or at your state's fish and game agency website.

Some of the key regulations to know include the following:

- **Hunting season dates:** Make sure the waterfowl season is open.
- **Shooting times:** Good light is needed when shooting. Find out when it is legal to shoot in the morning and how late you can shoot in the evening.
- **Bag limits:** Different species of ducks and geese have different limits for how many birds you can harvest in a day.

Fair Chase

Good hunters follow a code of ethics beyond what's in a regulations booklet. Ethics means doing the right thing, even when others can't see what you're doing. It means hunting in a way that is fair to the animal and to other hunters.

Only shoot at birds you feel confident about hitting.

Good ethics include hunting with fair chase methods. For instance, don't shoot at game that's too far away. You might cripple the waterfowl. Take careful shots that give you a good chance of hitting your target. Work hard to find the ducks and geese you shoot. A hunting dog can be a big help in finding your downed game.

A hunting dog will help you get your bird from the water.

CHAPTER FIVE

LET'S GO HUNTING!

Are you ready to go hunting? Waterfowl hunting requires special gear and equipment. Then you need to know good strategies for hunting ducks and geese.

Shotgun

Many hunters use a 12-gauge or a 20-gauge shotgun for hunting waterfowl. The gauge is the measurement of the inside diameter of the barrel. Both shotguns are loaded with a shell that includes a case that holds powder and shot pellets. When a hunter fires the shell, the pellets spread out and hit the game.

Steel Shot Shells

You must hunt ducks or geese with steel or other nontoxic shot. Lead is illegal because waterfowl and other wildlife might accidentally eat pellets that drop in the water. Animals that eat these pellets can die from lead poisoning.

Shotgun shell

12-gauge shotgun

Duck call

Decoys

Decoys are usually made of plastic or cork. Hunters usually put decoys in the water or the field near where they are hunting. A string attached to a weight is tied to each water decoy, so the decoys won't float away. The decoys look like ducks or geese floating in the water. When real birds see the decoys, they think the water or the field is a safe place to land.

Duck and Goose Calls

Most hunters use duck and goose calls. These are mouth-operated instruments that you blow in to sound like ducks or geese. Duck and goose calls are usually made of wood or plastic. A lot of practice is needed to make a good duck or goose call. When hunting, match your calling style to the waterfowl you're hunting.

Boats

Many waterfowl hunters walk or wade to their hunting spot. Some hunters use special boats or canoes that can navigate very shallow water. Some states don't allow certain kinds of boats, so make sure you check your state's rules. Always wear a life jacket, even if you know how to swim!

Hunters climb into a pit blind.

Hunting Blinds

A blind hides you from flying ducks or geese as they approach your hunting spot. When the birds are in range, you surprise them and take your shot. A blind can be as simple as a hiding place in the brush or behind a tree stump. You might bring some camouflage (dark multicolored fabric) and set up a temporary hideout. Some hunters build standing blinds made of wooden frames with cattails and brush woven around them. Camouflage netting over the top stops birds from seeing hunters from above.

Field hunters often use layout blinds. Layout blinds have spring-loaded doors that cover you until it's time to sit up to shoot. Some field hunters enjoy pit blinds dug into the ground with benches to sit on. When ducks or geese approach, the hunter stands up and shoots.

When hunting ducks or geese, wear clothes that will keep you warm and dry in the cool fall weather.

Clothes

Duck and goose hunters wear clothes that keep them warm and dry and hide them from waterfowl. Birds will fly away if they spot a hunter, so these warm clothes should blend into the scenery. Most waterfowl hunters do not wear blaze orange while they hunt, because ducks and geese would see the color and avoid the hunter's spot. However, you can wear blaze orange while walking or boating to and from your hunting spot. Some states require a small amount of blaze orange clothing, so check your state's rules. Bring waterproof gloves to wear as you place and pick up decoys from cold water. Waders or hip boots are tall waterproof boots that keep you from getting wet as you hike through marshes and wetlands. In waterfowl season, the water is too cold to stand in without waterproof boots.

A good retrieving dog can be a hunter's best friend.

Accessories

Since waterfowl hunting starts in the early morning, you may need a headlamp, or a light that you wear on your head or cap, for getting to your hunting spot in the dark. You should have a bag or a strap to carry your game. Have a knife and game shears (a type of scissors) ready for when it's time to breast out (clean) your bird.

Waterfowl Hunting Dogs

Dogs are important helpers for waterfowl hunters. You can train your dog to swim out and get ducks or geese that you shoot. Training a good waterfowl dog is challenging but very rewarding. Good dog breeds for duck and goose hunting include Labrador retrievers and Chesapeake Bay retrievers or even smaller dogs such as Boykin spaniels. But any dog that likes the water and retrieving can become a good duck or goose dog!

Hunting Ducks

There are two main types of ducks—puddle ducks and diving ducks. Diving ducks, such as canvasbacks and scaups, dive below the water's surface to feed. They eat underwater plants, bugs, and small animals. Diving ducks like deeper water, so hunting them can be a challenge.

Puddle ducks tip up to feed.

Puddle ducks—such as mallards, wood ducks, or teal—dip their heads in shallow water to feed. They usually do not dive down for their food. Their hind ends usually stay above the water as they tip up. Puddle ducks are easy to find and fun to hunt. You might even get multiple species on the same hunt.

The basic duck call is a mallard call. But smart hunters carry different kinds of duck calls around their necks. There are calls for many different species of ducks. Duck language sounds include hails (greetings), quacks, chuckles, feeding purrs, and more. Some hunters put out diving duck decoys, then hide in boats that lie very flat to the water's surface. When diving ducks fly close, the hunter shoots.

Decoy Spread for Diving Ducks

Make a "v" leading to where you hide.

Decoy Spread for Puddle Ducks

Make an opening for ducks to attempt to land in.

You don't need a boat or blind to duck hunt. If you walk quietly through a marsh, you might find a duck to flush.

Another good method for hunting ducks is jump shooting. Walk quietly along a creek or up to a pond or a wetland. When a duck sees you, it will flush (fly away quickly) and give you the chance to shoot. You can also float in a canoe or boat, so long as the boat's motor is not under power. One hunter steers the watercraft, and the other hunter sits in front looking for ducks. When a duck flushes, take your shot.

Hunting Geese

Geese are hunted on the water and also in fields where they come to eat. A harvested grainfield or hayfield makes a great place to hunt geese on land. Set up standing decoys in the field to look like a flock of geese. Then hide among the decoys in a layout or standing blind.

Use a goose call to try to attract flying geese. Goose calls are made for Canada geese, snow geese, and white-fronted geese (usually called specklebellies). Each species makes different sounds. Goose language includes honks, groans, clucks, and double clucks. When the geese hear your calls and see your decoys, they might fly in to take a closer look. When the geese are close, take your shot.

To hunt for geese on the water, put out floating decoys and hide in brush or a blind. Call to attract passing geese. You will probably have the best luck calling to a single goose or geese in a pair, rather than a large flock.

Goose hunting often takes place in a field away from water.

WATERFOWL GUIDE

MALLARD

Mallards are big puddle ducks, weighing about 3 pounds (1.3 kilograms). They usually live in or near shallow water such as wetlands. These ducks are very shy and can be challenging to hunt, especially late in the season.

GREEN-WINGED TEAL

Teal are small, fast-flying puddle ducks. The green-winged teal is a common species of teal in North America. They usually fly in groups that twist and turn rapidly. They are the smallest ducks, and usually weigh less than 1 pound (0.5 kg).

WOOD DUCK

Wood ducks prefer habitats with shallow water and lots of trees. Unlike most other ducks that nest on the ground, woods ducks nest in tree holes. These puddle ducks weigh about 1 pound (0.5 kg).

SCAUP

A scaup is a diving duck often known as a bluebill. They prefer fresh water, such as rivers, lakes, or wetlands. Scaups weigh about 2 pounds (0.9 kg).

CANVASBACK

Canvasbacks are diving ducks that are popular with hunters. These ducks can weigh up to 4 pounds (1.8 kg). Canvasbacks like shallow water, such as ponds, in the summer. They spend the winter in protected lakes and saltwater bays.

CANADA GOOSE

Canada geese can live almost anywhere. They can be found from mountain habitats to city parks, as long as there is nearby water. There are several kinds of Canada geese. These can range from 3-pound (1.3-kg) cacklers to giants that weigh 12 pounds (5.4 kg) or more.

SNOW GOOSE

Snow geese nest in the Arctic during the summer. In the winter, they migrate south to shallow water, such as saltwater and freshwater marshes. They frequently feed in wheat and other farm fields. Lesser snow geese weigh 4 to 6 pounds (1.8 to 2.7 kg). Greater snow geese usually weigh 4 to 8 pounds (1.8 to 3.6 kg).

HOW TO PREPARE YOUR BIRD

Ducks and geese are delicious to eat. The meat is red, rich, and juicy. But to have delicious meals, you have to know how to properly clean and cook your game.

Plucking

Holding the bird by a hind leg or a wing, pull off all the feathers from the body and leg. Use a knife to cut off the duck's head and feet. Use game shears to snip up either side of the spine. Remove the backbone and guts. When the bird is clean, wash it in cold water.

In addition to being fun to hunt, waterfowl tastes great!

Breasting Out

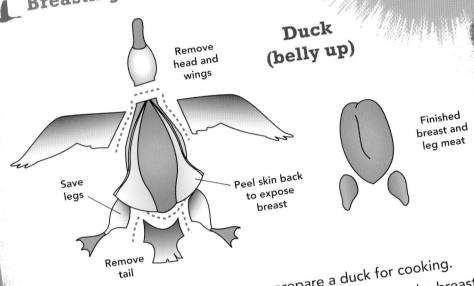

Duck (belly up)

Remove head and wings

Save legs

Peel skin back to expose breast

Remove tail

Finished breast and leg meat

Breasting out is an easy way to prepare a duck for cooking. Strip the skin with feathers from the breast. Cut out the breast meat on either side of the middle bone of the breast. Now you have meat that is ready for roasting or other cooking methods.

Roasting Waterfowl

One of the best ways to cook a duck is to roast it. Roll a plucked duck in seasoned flour and brown it on all sides in a skillet with hot oil. Remove the duck meat and sauté an onion in the skillet. Put the sautéed onion in a roasting pan, lay the duck on top (breast up), cover with aluminum foil, and roast at 250°F (120°C) for two hours for small ducks or three or four hours for large ducks or geese.

GLOSSARY

CONSERVATION

the thoughtful, efficient, and careful use of natural resources

ETHICS

the way a hunter acts in the field that is fair to the animals and the sport

GAME SHEARS

a sturdy, scissorslike tool designed for cutting game

HABITAT

the place an animal lives, including its cover, food sources, and water

MIGRATE

to move from north to south in fall to escape cold or winter and back north in spring

NONTOXIC

not poisonous to animals or humans

SAFETY

a device on a firearm that keeps it from accidentally firing

SPECIES

animals that are grouped together by scientists because they are related

LERNER *e* SOURCE™

Expand learning beyond the printed book. Download free, complementary educational resources for this book from our website, www.lerneresource.com.

FOR MORE INFORMATION

Further Reading

Johnson, Rebecca L. *A Journey into a Lake*. Minneapolis: Lerner Publications Company, 2004.

Landau, Elaine. *Labrador Retrievers Are the Best!* Minneapolis: Lerner Publications Company, 2010.

Lerner, Carol. *On the Wing: American Birds in Migration*. New York: HarperCollins Publishers, 2001.

Websites

Junior Shooters
http://www.juniorshooters.net/
This website features information on hunting clubs, events, and safety geared toward young shooters.

U.S. Fish & Wildlife Service—Let's Go Outside
http://www.fws.gov/letsgooutside/kids.html
This website has games and information about protecting animal habitats.

Waterfowl Identification
http://www.ducks.org/hunting/waterfowl-id
This website features photos and calls of different ducks to teach hunters the different waterfowl species.

INDEX

About the Author

Tom Carpenter has hunted and fished across North America for almost five decades, pursuing big game, waterfowl, upland birds, wild turkeys, small game, and fish of all kinds. He has raised three sons as sportsmen and written countless articles and contributed to dozens of books on hunting, fishing, nature, and the outdoors.